JOURNEY THROUGH SPAIN

ANITA GANERI

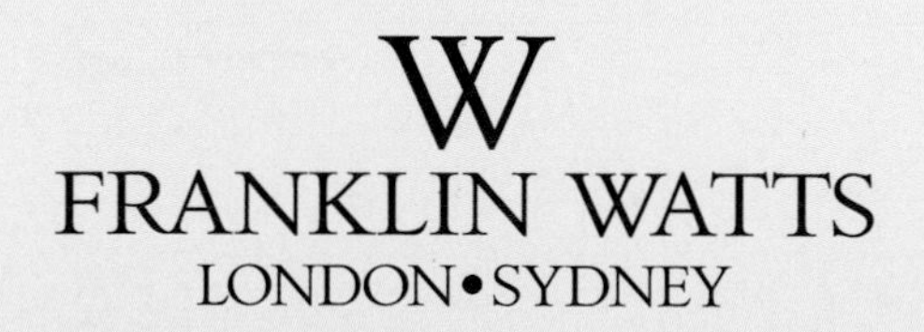

W
FRANKLIN WATTS
LONDON•SYDNEY

Franklin Watts
Published in Great Britain in 2017 by The Watts Publishing Group

Credits
Editor in Chief: John Miles
Series Editor: Amy Stephenson
Series Designer: Emma DeBanks
Picture Researcher: Diana Morris

Picture Credits: agefotostock/Superstock: 7tr, 14, 18-19b. Alexandrpeers/Dreamstime: 6bl. Steve Allen/Dreamstime: 7cl. Manuel Garcia Alonso/Fotoyos: 9cr. Amibumping/Dreamstime: 8-9c. Arenaphotouk/Dreamstime: 4, 20c. Phillip Armitage/Dreamstime: 27t. Richard Banary/Dreamstime: 7br, 29c. Mark Baynes/Alamy: 9br. Ekaterina Belova/Dreamstime: 7bcr, 26b. Justin Black/Dreamstime: front cover. Borjalaria/Dreamstime: 6cl. Dan Breckwoldt/Dreamstime: 6c, 15t. Mauricio Jordan de Souza Coelho/Dreamstime: 28b. Alan Dawson/Alamy: 19t. dibrova/Shutterstock: 6bc.Dinozzaver/Dreamstime: 7tc. Dennis Dolkens/Dreamstime: 15b. j g fabregas/Wikimedia Commons: 11c. Iakov Filimonov/Dreamstime: 17t. Food-micro/Dreamstime: 17b. Anthony Hathaway/Dreamstime: 5t. Hronek/Dreamstime: 23t. Gaspar Janos/Shutterstock: 24b. Juliann/Shutterstock: 6tl. Denys Kurylow/Dreamstime: 7tl. Rafael Laguillo/Dreamstime: 19c. Lunamarina/Dreamstime: 7bra, 24t. Neil Machin/Dreamstime: 9tr. Marlee/Dreamstime: 6tc. Juan Moyano/Dreamstime: 16c. Juan Carlos Muñoz/agefotostock/Superstock: 10. Natursports/Dreamstime: 13t, 27b. Odna/Dreamstime: 7tlb. Parkinsonsniper/Dreamstime: 7cb. peresanz/Shutterstock: 1, 27c. Pixattitude/Dreamstime: 7bl. Ganna Poltoratska/Dreamstime: 7bc. Glen Price/Dreamstime: 17c. Rido/Dreamstime: 6cr. Saaaaa/Dreamstime: 3, 20-21b, 25b. Roman Sigaev/Fotolia: 5b. Stanko07/Dreamstime: 25t. Steveng1892/Dreamstime: 12b. Nick Stubbs/Dreamstime: 23c. Richard Thomas/Dreamstime: 7cr. Anibal Trejo/Dreamstime: 7c. Carlos Violda/Shutterstock: 11b. Vvoevale/Dreamstime: 16b. Tim de Waele: 22b. Sebastian Wasek/agefotostock/Superstock: 11t. Piotr Wawrzniuk/Dreamstime: 29t. Adam Wells/adamwells.com: 13b. Peter Wey/Dreamstime: 6br. sonya zhuravetc/Fotolia: 21c.

Dewey number: 946
ISBN: 978 1 4451 3663 9

Printed in China

Franklin Watts
An imprint of
Hachette Children's Group
Part of The Watts Publishing Group
Carmelite House
50 Victoria Embankment
London EC4Y 0DZ

An Hachette UK Company
www.hachette.co.uk

www.franklinwatts.co.uk

CONTENTS

BIENVENIDOS A ESPAÑA!

Bienvenidos a España! Welcome to Spain! Covering an area of around 506,000 sq km, Spain is a large country in south-west Europe. It has a long and rich history, stunning scenery, and a fascinating culture. When you think of Spain, you might imagine bullfighting, flamenco dancing and football but there's much more to this beautiful country than that. On this journey, you'll be riding a camel across a volcanic landscape, kayaking around the coast, throwing tomatoes at a fiesta, and lots more besides.

▼ A patchwork of olive trees covers a hillside in Andalucía, southern Spain.

Sand, sun and sea

Separated from the rest of Europe (except Portugal) by the Pyrenees mountains, Spain stretches south to the Mediterranean Sea. To the north, it has borders with France and Andorra; to the west, with Portugal. Two groups of islands – the Balearics and the Canaries – lie off the coast. Spain's climate and landscape vary from snow-capped peaks to sun-drenched beaches. Whether you fancy a challenging hike or a relaxing swim, Spain has something for everyone.

▲ The Pyrenees mountains.

Story of Spain

Over the centuries, many different cultures – among them the Phoenicians, Greeks, Carthaginians and Romans – have all left their mark on Spain. In the 8th century CE, Muslims from North Africa invaded and ruled much of Spain for hundreds of years. Later, Spanish explorers sailed far and wide, conquering large parts of the 'New World'. In the 20th century, Spain survived dictatorships, military uprisings and civil war, but today, Spain is a modern democracy and a leading country in the world.

Spanish life

Spain is a big country and the way people live varies from region to region. In general, though, Spanish people are sociable and family-orientated. Food plays an important part in their lives and they like to meet up and eat together. You can find cafés and restaurants everywhere, serving delicious tapas, paella and other Spanish specialities.

▶ A sign for directions to the city of Alicante in both Spanish and Catalan.

Habla español?

Do you speak Spanish? Spanish is the official language of Spain but many other languages and dialects are also spoken, including Catalan, Galician and English in the tourist resorts. Around the world, Spanish is also spoken in countries such as Mexico and Peru, where Spanish explorers settled. In fact, there are more Spanish speakers worldwide than speakers of any other language apart from Mandarin Chinese.

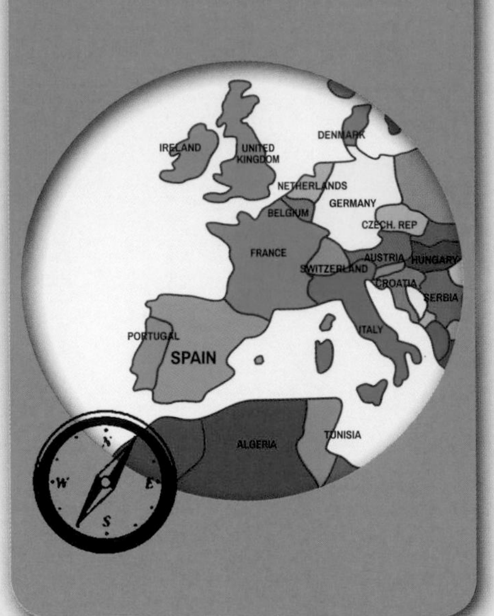

JOURNEY PLANNER

Atlantic Ocean

1

2

KEY

- your route around Spain
- flight / ferry
- river
- road
- capital city

Canary Islands
LA PALMA
LANZAROTE
Mount Teide
FUERTEVENTURA
4
Santa Cruz
LA GOMERA
TENERIFE
Las Palmas
FRONTERA
GRAND CANARIA

Atlantic Ocean

A Coruña
Gijón
Oviedo
Santiago de Compostela
León
Ourense
Salamanca
PORTUGAL
Cáceres
Badajoz
Mérida
Huelva
Seville
Coto Doñana
Jerez
Cádiz
Gibraltar
Algeciras

3
4
Bay of Biscay
Ribadesella
Santander
Bilbao
1
San Sebastian
FRANCE
Sotres
Picos de Europa
Vitoria-Gasteiz
Pamplona
ANDORRA
Burgos
Logrono
Palencia
Valladolid
Zaragoza
Fraga
5
Barcelona
Coca
2
Segovia
Tarragona
Ávila
MADRID
3
MENORCA
Cuenca
Mediterranean Sea
Soller
6
Toledo
Cuevas de Drach
Buñol
Valencia
Palma
IBIZA
Coudad Real
Albacete
Elx
Alicante
Córdoba
Murcia
Jaén
Lorca
Cartagena
Granada
Sierra Nevada
6
Almeria
Málaga
5
Strait of Gibraltar

BILBAO TO RIBADESELLA

A brilliant place to start your journey through Spain is the city of Bilbao on the north coast. From Britain, you can reach Bilbao by ferry, but take some sea sickness tablets with you. The Bay of Biscay gets pretty choppy, especially if you're travelling in winter. Bilbao is one of Spain's biggest ports, and spreads out along the River Nervión. Take your pick from one of the city's many bridges to cross from one bank to another. The Zubizuri ('White Bridge') has a walkway of see-through glass bricks.

▼ The striking architecture of the Guggenheim Museum links into Bilbao's industrial and shipbuilding past.

Guggenheim Museum

For years, Bilbao was known as an industrial city, famous for shipbuilding and the export of iron from nearby quarries, but the opening of the Guggenheim Museum in 1997 has put it firmly on the tourist map. The outside of the building has spectacular, curved walls, made from stone, glass and titanium, and is designed to catch the light. Inside, there are 19 galleries to wander around, showing thousands of works of modern art.

Ribadesella by rail

From Bilbao, catch a FEVE tourist train for a scenic ride along the coast to Ribadesella. This pretty little seaside town is split into two parts, on either side of an estuary. On one side is the old seaport, below a clifftop church. On the other is a holiday resort with a large, sandy beach. On the edge of the town, you can visit the Cueva de Tito Bustillo. This cave is famous for its prehistoric cave paintings, which date from around 18,000 BCE.

▲ The estuary at Ribadesella.

Canoeing

Every year, in August, the Sella International Descent takes place in Ribadesella. It's a world-famous canoe race along the River Sella, and hundreds of paddlers take part. If you fancy getting some practice in for next year's race, head upstream to Arriondas where you can hire a canoe and a life jacket.

▲ Taking part in the Sella International Descent on the River Sella.

Basque culture

Bilbao is the largest city in a region of Spain called the Basque Country. The Basque people are very proud of their region and culture. Along with Spanish, they speak their own language, called Basque (or Euskera). They also have their own traditions and sports, such as *pelota*. This is a game where teams hit a ball against a wall, then catch it with their hands, wooden bats or wicker baskets.

◀ Traditional Basque costume and dancing.

THE PICOS DE EUROPA

From Ribadesella, hop on a bus for the short ride to the picturesque village of Sotres. It is nestled among the Picos de Europa mountains, with their stunning peaks, rushing rivers and plunging gorges. The name of the mountains means 'Peaks of Europe'. It is said that they were named by returning sailors in the 15th and 16th centuries because they were the first glimpse that they had of home. The highest peak is Torre de Cerredo, which is 2,650 m high.

Walking tour

Around two million visitors come to the Picos de Europa and the best way to see them is on foot. Sotres makes an ideal base for a walking tour. It's on the route of the GR-71 footpath, which is part of a vast network of long-distance footpaths criss-crossing Europe. Look out for the markers (white and red stripes) on posts and trees and you won't get lost. Sotres itself is the highest village in the Picos, and home to the famous Cabrales blue cheese, which is matured in the nearby caves.

▶ The small village of Sotres has a population of fewer than 150 people.

Cares Gorge

The Garganta del Cares (Cares Gorge) is a dramatic gorge, 1 km deep and 12 km long, carved out by the River Cares. High mountains rise up on either side. To get the best view, follow the dramatic path cut into the side of the mountains. The path is narrow so you need to watch your step and keep away from the edge – it's a long way down.

▲ The Cares Trail runs alongside the River Cares and is the most popular hiking trail in the Picos.

Picu Urriellu

For a real challenge, head for Picu Urriellu, a jagged, tooth-shaped peak. The west face of the mountain has one of the most difficult rock climbs in the world. Climbers have to scramble their way up a sheer rock wall around 500 m high using ropes, or 'free' climbing with only their hands and feet.

▼ Most of the mountains in the Picos, including Picu Urriellu, are formed from limestone.

Picos park

The Picos de Europa is Europe's largest national park, with many protected animals. Grab your binoculars and see how many of them you can spot on your trek:

- Capercaillie
- Lammergeier
- Iberian wolf
- Cantabrian brown bear
- Pyrenean chamois
- Spanish ibex
- Alpine chough

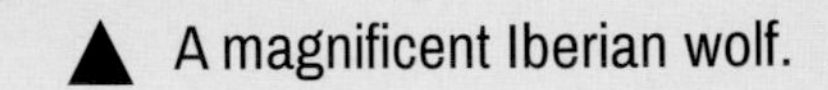

▲ A magnificent Iberian wolf.

RIBADESELLA TO SANTIAGO DE COMPOSTELA

The easiest way to reach Santiago de Compostela is to head back to Ribadesella and catch another FEVE train. Alternatively, you could join thousands of other walkers on the *Camino del Norte*, (Northern Route) an ancient pilgrimage route along the north coast. The route is about 825 km long and takes 5–6 weeks to complete, but you will join it about half-way along. It's hilly, so you need to be reasonably fit, but you'll be rewarded with amazing views of the Picos on one side and the sea on the other.

Santiago de Compostela

In the Middle Ages, Santiago de Compostela was the third holiest place in Christianity, after Jerusalem and Rome. Pilgrims flocked here from all over Europe. According to legend, the body of Saint James, one of Christ's disciples, was buried in Santiago in 813 CE. A cathedral was later built on the spot where his remains were found.

▼ Many hikers on the Camino del Norte carry backpacks, as shelters along the route are 20–30 km apart.

▶ The impressive towers of the western entrance to Santiago Cathedral are a welcome sight for weary hikers.

Santiago Cathedral

The twin towers of Santiago Cathedral soar over the Praza do Obradoiro, a huge square in the centre of the city. The building dates from the 11–12th centuries but stands on the site of an earlier shrine. As you go in, take a look at the *Pórtico da Gloria* (Doorway of Glory), with its beautifully carved figures and Bible scenes. See if you can spot the carving of Maestro Mateo, the sculptor of the doorway, below the statue of Saint James. Pilgrims touch the carving of Maestro Mateo with their foreheads for luck and wisdom.

Galicia

The region around Santiago is called Galicia and is well worth taking a look around. Bordering the Atlantic Ocean, it has fine old towns, sandy bays and forest-covered hills. Fishing is a major industry for the coastal areas, so head to Noia, or one of the other fishing villages along the coast, to sample some local fish and seafood. *Polvo à feira* (boiled octopus) is a traditional Galician dish.

Religion in Spain

About 70 per cent of Spanish people are Roman Catholic Christians, although many do not attend church regularly. The Romans introduced Christianity to Spain about 2,000 years ago but, in the 8th century CE, Islam was brought to Spain by Muslims from North Africa, known as the Moors. The Moors were driven out by the 15th century CE and Spain became Christian again.

CAPITULUM hujus Almae Apostolicae et Metropolitanae Ecclesiae Compostellanae sigilli Altaris Beati Jacobi Apostoli custos, ut omnibus Fidelibus et Peregrinis ex toto terrarum Orbe, devotionis affectu vel voti causa, ad limina Apostoli Nostri Hispaniarum Patroni ac Tutelaris **SANCTI JACOBI** *convenientibus, authenticas visitationis litteras expediat, omnibus et singulis praesentes inspecturis, notum facit: Dnum.*
Adamum Davidem WELLS
hoc sacratissimum Templum pietatis causa devote visitasse. In quorum fidem praesentes litteras, sigillo ejusdem Sanctae Ecclesiae munitas, ei confero.
Datum Compostellae die 27 *mensis* Maii
anno Dni 2011.

SIGILLUM • CAPITULI • BEATI • JACOBI • COMPOSTELLAE

Canonicus Deputatus pro Peregrinis

◀ Pilgrims who complete their journey to Santiago are given a certificate as a record of their pilgrimage.

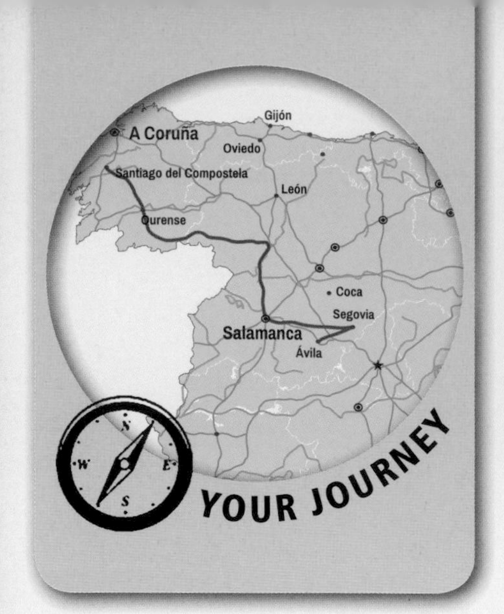

SANTIAGO DE COMPOSTELA TO SALAMANCA

There's no direct train from Santiago de Compostela to Salamanca but you can drive or take a bus. The bus journey lasts about seven hours and takes you through the vast region of central Spain, called the *meseta* (plateau). Much of the meseta is covered by fields of crops, vineyards and olive groves, or dry, dusty plains. This region is also rich in history, with many stunning castles and cathedrals.

University town

Salamanca was a Roman town before being conquered by the Moors (see page 13). It is home to many historic buildings made from sandstone, which glows gold and pink in the sun. Salamanca University dates back to 1250 and is one of the oldest universities in Europe. If you fancy becoming a student, you can enrol on a Spanish course. Thousands of international students study Spanish here every year, which gives the town a diverse population. The Spanish spoken in Salamanca is the most pure and accent-free in Spain.

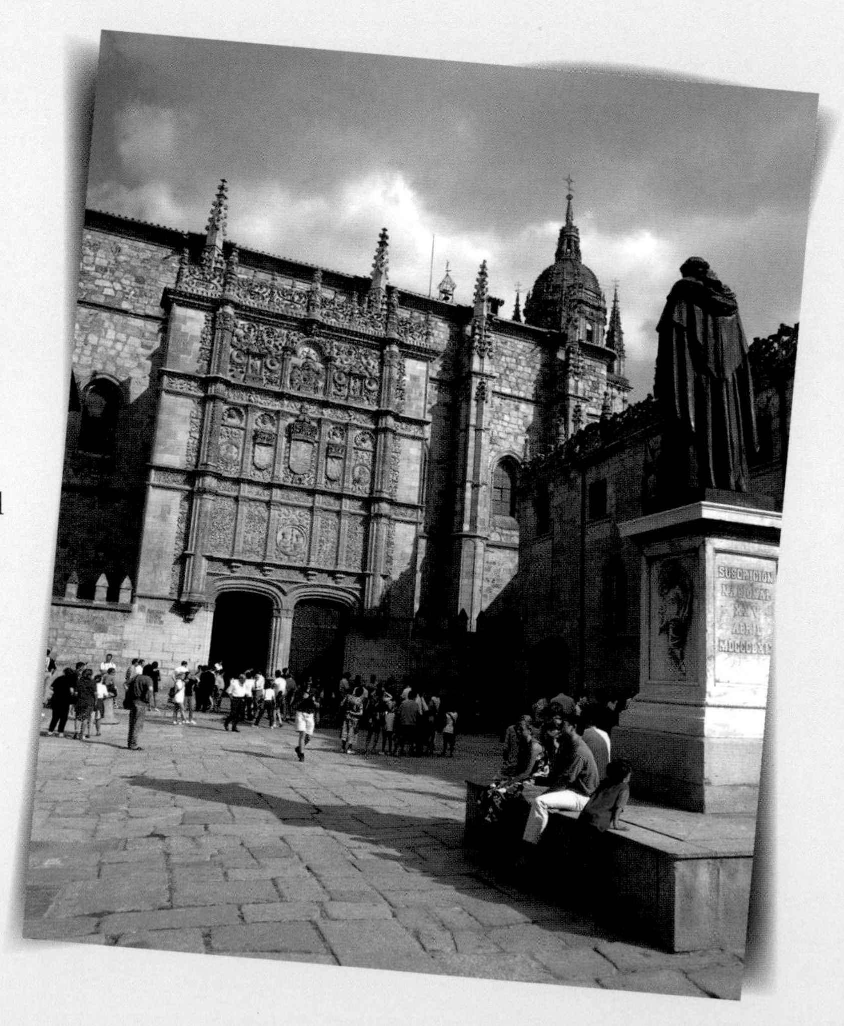

A statue of famous writer and translator, Luis de Léon, faces the University of Salamanca.

▶ Segovia's fairy-tale castle was originally a fortress and is now a museum.

Castles of Castile

Another bus ride will take you to Segovia where you can hop on board a hot-air balloon for a bird's-eye view of the city. Marvel at the spectacular castle, which looks as if it comes straight out of a fairy tale. Then take in the Roman aqueduct, which was built 2,000 years ago and is still in brilliant condition. The tour takes about three hours and comes with a guide to explain the sights, and with lunch after the flight.

Medieval walls

About an hour's drive away from Segovia is the city of Ávila, famous for its medieval city walls. Built in the 11th century, the walls are more than 2 km long and have 88 semi-circular turrets and nine gateways. A walkway runs along them for about half of their length.

Other places to visit

León Cathedral – Look out for its magnificent stained glass windows, showing saints and scenes from Bible stories.

Cuenca – Famous for its 'Hanging Houses' that jut out precariously above the gorge along which the town is built.

Castillo de Coca – This beautiful castle is made from rose-coloured bricks and was the home of a wealthy local family.

Mérida – Spanish people love being entertained and the city's Roman theatre is one of the finest in the world. It is still used for a summer drama festival.

▲ The aqueduct in Segovia was in use until the late 19th century.

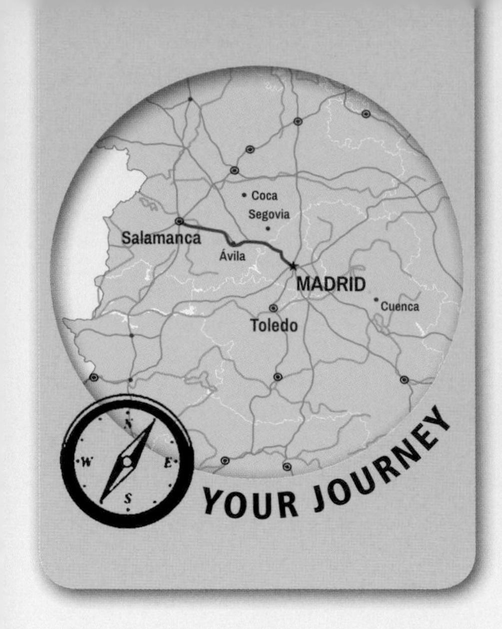

SALAMANCA TO MADRID

Spain has one of the longest motorway networks in the world, and you can drive from Salamanca to Madrid along A and AP roads. You have to pay to use AP roads so have some change handy. It's a distance of about 215 km, and the journey takes around 2.5 hours. When you reach the city, look out for the Kilometre Zero in Puerta del Sol, Madrid's central square. It marks the centre of Spain's road network.

About Madrid

Madrid is the capital of Spain, and the biggest city. It is located almost right in the middle of Spain, on the banks of the River Manzanares. The city is home to around 3.3 million people, known as *madrileños*, but is visited by millions of tourists each year. They come to enjoy the beautiful buildings, such as those that line the Plaza Mayor (below), thriving art scene, fabulous food, and more. Madrid has more trees and green spaces than any other city in Europe, and also has Spain's largest bullring.

▲ Kilometre Zero in Puerta del Sol.

Sightseeing tour

There are many ways of seeing the sights of Madrid but for something slightly different, book on to a rooftop walking tour. It lasts around three hours and your local guide leads you up onto five rooftops for stunning views of the city. Learn all about the city's history and look out for some of its most famous buildings, such as the *Palacio Real* (Royal Palace) and the Prado Museum.

▲ The Prado Museum houses one of the world's finest European art collections.

Snack stop

If all that sightseeing makes you hungry, there are plenty of places to stop for a snack. Try some delicious *churros* with chocolate. Churros are crispy doughnut sticks, traditionally dunked into a cup of thick hot chocolate. Spain is also famous for tapas – small dishes of food that can be served hot or cold (see below).

◀ Crispy sticks of churros.

Ten traditional tapas

Tortilla a la española – Spanish omelette

Patatas bravas – fried potatoes in spicy tomato sauce

Jamón serrano – thin slices of ham

Queso manchego – sheep's milk cheese

Ensalada de pimientos rojos – salad of roasted red peppers

Calamares fritos – deep fried squid rings

Albóndigas – meatballs in tomato sauce

Gambas a la plancha – whole grilled prawns

Chorizo – sausage flavoured with garlic and paprika

Pollo al ajillo – chicken in garlic sauce

▲ A delicious selection of traditional tapas.

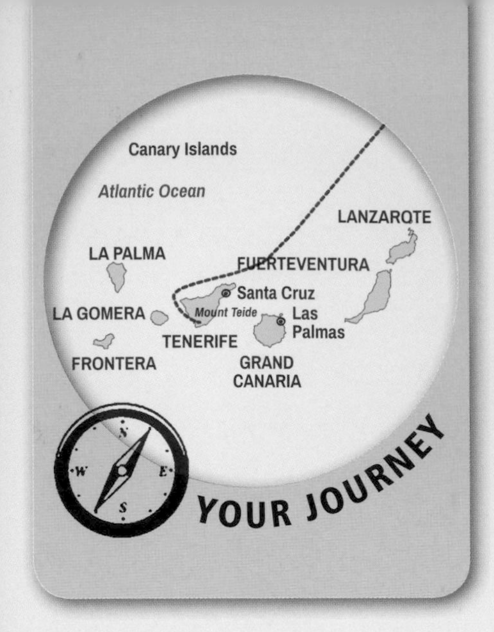

MADRID TO TENERIFE

The Canary Islands lie in the Atlantic Ocean off the north-west coast of Africa. They are the tips of underwater volcanoes that erupted from the seabed millions of years ago. There are seven large islands, and several smaller ones, all with spectacular scenery and sunny weather, making them popular places for holidays. From Madrid, the flight to Tenerife, the largest of the islands, takes about three hours.

Mount Teide

Tenerife's most striking feature is Mount Teide, a dormant volcano that last erupted in 1909. At 3,718 m tall, it's also Spain's highest mountain. You can reach the top by cable car in just eight minutes, or you can put on your boots and hike up along a path, called *La Rambleta*. Look out for the amazing rock formations, including *Los Huevos del Teide* ('The Eggs of Teide') – giant black balls of lava. It takes about five hours to reach the summit – you need a permit for the final climb – but it's worth the effort for the spectacular views. On a clear day, you can see right across to the other Canary Islands.

▶ The tall, cone shape of Mount Teide is typical of a composite volcano.

Volcano park

From Tenerife you can catch a ferry to Lanzarote, the island furthest to the east and north of the Canaries. In the 18th century, more than 100 volcanoes erupted on the island of Lanzarote. Lava buried 11 villages but, luckily, no one was killed. Today, these volcanoes, known as the *Montañas del Fuego* ('Fire Mountains'), form part of Timanfaya National Park. You can take a bus trip around the area, or ride a camel across the volcanic landscape. Afterwards, stop for lunch at a restaurant where the food is cooked using geothermal heat.

▲ A man from La Gomera demonstrating *El Silbo.*

▼ Tourists riding camels cross Timanfaya's volcanic landscape.

Whistle language

One of the smallest of the Canary Islands, La Gomera has a rugged landscape, which is criss-crossed by deep ravines and thick forests. In the past, this made communications difficult between villagers in different parts of the island. To solve the problem, they invented a language, called El Silbo, made up of whistling sounds. These sounds carry long distances from one valley to the next.

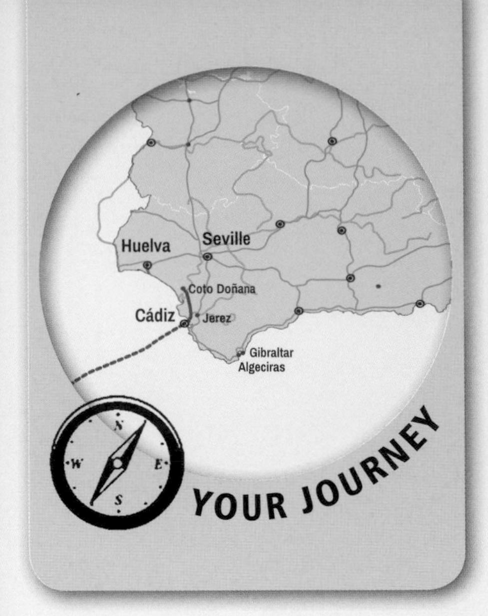

TENERIFE TO CÁDIZ

Head back to Tenerife to catch a ferry back to the mainland, landing at Cádiz in southern Spain. Cádiz has a long sea-faring history so you'll be in good company. In the 15th and 16th centuries, Christopher Columbus sailed from here to the New World. Cádiz is located on a spit of land that sticks out into the sea. Look out for the painted houses along the waterfront. Some have turrets from which look-outs kept watch for ships returning from the New World with their precious cargoes of gold.

White towns

The region around Cádiz is called Andalucia. Largely an agricultural area, it covers most of the southern part of Spain and stretches from the dry, dusty landscapes of Almería to the border with Portugal. Olives, cattle and various fruits are important to the economy of the area. Dotted around the hilltops are the *pueblos blancos* ('white towns'), with their clusters of whitewashed houses. The towns were built high in the hills as protection when the region was being fought over by the Moors and Christians.

▲ The white colour of the pueblos blancos helps keep the buildings cool by reflecting away the sun's heat.

Coto Doñana

A short drive from Cádiz is Coto Doñana National Park. The park is a huge stretch of marshes, beaches and sand dunes in the delta of the Guadalquivir River. It's home to a wealth of wildlife, including wild boar, flamingos and eagles. It's also one of the last places you can see the extremely rare Iberian lynx. See the park on an official guided tour, starting at the Acebuche visitor centre. The tour lasts for about four hours and you travel in a huge, four-wheel-drive bus. Book up beforehand – the number of visitors to the park is strictly controlled to protect the fragile environment.

Flamenco

More than just a dance, flamenco is a very famous part of Andalucian culture. It is lively, fiery and full of feeling. Wearing a traditional polka-dot dress and high-heeled shoes, a flamenco dancer beats out the rhythm with her heels, hands and by clicking a pair of castanets. She is accompanied by a guitar, a singer and loud shouts of '*Olé!*' from the audience. There is no strict choreography – dancers make up their own moves.

▶ A flamenco dancer strikes a dramatic pose.

▼ Cádiz is one of Europe's oldest cities, dating back to around 1100 BCE.

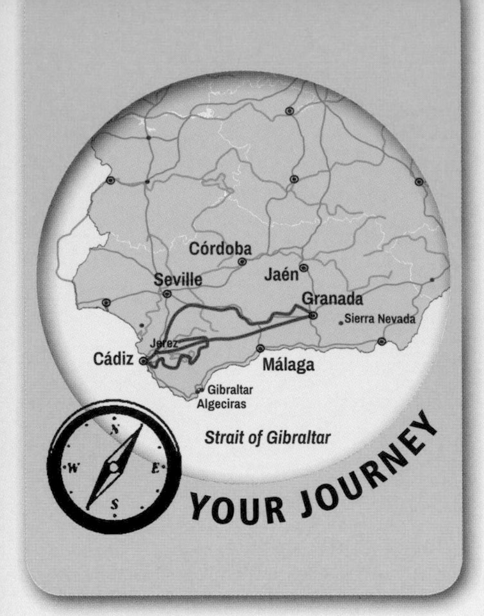

CÁDIZ TO GRANADA

La Vuelta is a top cycle race that takes place in Spain every year. It takes place over 23 days, with 21 day-long 'stages' and two rest days. If you're feeling energetic, you can ride the 2014 Stage 3 of la Vuelta from Cádiz to Arcos de la Frontera, a white town perched on a cliff. The ride is 190 km long and starts with a long, flat ride before a challenging series of hills. Head back to Cádiz so you can travel to Granada in style on board the *Al Andalus*, and watch Andalucía go by from the comfort of your own luxury train.

▼ The riders cycled past the Spanish navy ship *Juan Carlos I* at the start of Stage 3 of the 2014 la Vuelta.

Beautifully carved archways surround the Court of the Lions at the Alhambra Palace.

Granada

The city of Granada was conquered by the Moors (see page 13) in the 8th century and, for the next 600 years, it was one of the most important cities in Muslim Spain. It fell to the Christian rulers, King Ferdinand and Queen Isabella, in 1492. To get a feel for the city's Moorish past, stroll through the narrow lanes of El Albaicín (old Moorish quarter). Many churches were built over the city's mosques but you can still see many houses with Moorish decorations and Moorish baths.

The Alhambra Palace

The dazzling Alhambra Palace draws thousands of visitors to Granada each year. Built by the Moors from the 13th century, its beautiful halls, pavilions and gardens were created as a paradise on Earth. Tours begin in the part of the palace called the *Palacios Nazaríes*, with its exquisitely carved archways and ceilings. Don't miss the Court of the Lions, (see above), its spectacular fountain rests on the back of 12 marble lions.

A snowboarder at one of the ski resorts in the Sierra Nevada mountains.

Sierra Nevada

The Sierra Nevada mountain range runs through Andalucia and has 14 peaks higher than 3,000 m. Many of the peaks are covered in snow in winter, making this a very popular spot with skiers. One of Europe's highest roads – the GR411 – runs past the ski resort of Sol y Nieve where you can ski, snowboard or soak up the sun.

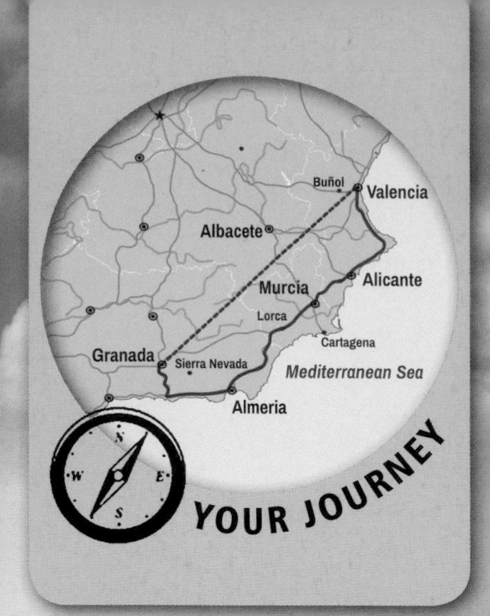

GRANADA TO VALENCIA

The quickest way to travel from Granada to Valencia is by plane, but you'll see more of eastern Spain by car. The journey is around 520 km and takes about five hours. You'll drive mainly along the E15, part of the international road network that runs right the way from Scotland through Europe to Spain. Break your journey with a stop at one of the sandy beaches along the Costa Blanca.

▲ Sparkling blue waters and sandy beaches are typical of resorts along the Costa Blanca.

▼ Penyal d'Ifac rising out of the sea.

Costa Blanca

Stretching for 200 km along eastern Spain is the Costa Blanca ('White Coast'), a popular spot for holidaymakers with resorts such as Alicante, Benidorm and Dénia. From Benidorm, head north to Penyal d'Ifac, a huge limestone rock that seems to rise straight out of the sea. Walk up the path to a tunnel dug through the rock. On the other side, it's a scramble to the summit so make sure that you wear proper shoes.

Fiesta time!

A good time to visit Valencia is March, when the city holds a spectacular fiesta (festival), to commemorate Saint Joseph. Each neighbourhood produces a *falla* – a huge puppet, filled with firecrackers. A falla can take up to a year to build from paper, wax and wood. The fiesta lasts for five days and nights, with a party every night. On the last night, the fallas are paraded through the streets, then set alight in a spectacular display.

La Tomatina

Another fantastic fiesta takes place each August in the village of Buñol, near Valencia, when thousands of visitors pelt each other with ripe tomatoes. The festival is called La Tomatina and is thought to have begun as a fight between local children in 1945. Trucks bring more than 100 tonnes of tomatoes for people to hurl. The fight lasts for exactly one hour.

▲ Paella being cooked over an open fire.

Perfect paella

Valencia is home to Spain's most famous dish – paella. Every family has its own recipe. Paella is made from rice mixed with peppers, beans, chicken, pork and rabbit. It can also be made with seafood. It is cooked in a large pan over an open fire. For the best paella, head for the village of El Palmar, just outside the city. This is where paella rice is grown.

▼ A crowd gathers around an elaborate falla before it is set alight.

VALENCIA TO BARCELONA

If there's one place in Spain that you don't want to miss it's the city of Barcelona, the capital of Catalonia. Its official languages are Catalan, Spanish and Aranese. It has amazing buildings, delicious food, world-famous football, markets and shops and a beautiful beach. Take the train from Valencia – it takes around three hours. To get around the city, walk, take the metro or hop on a bus or bike.

Sagrada Família

The most famous sight in Barcelona is the Sagrada Família, an amazing church designed by the architect Antoni Gaudí. The church was his life's work and he lived on the site for 16 years. When Gaudí died in 1926, he was buried in the crypt. Building still continues today, and is officially due to be finished in 2026. Enter through the Nativity Façade, carved with scenes from Jesus' birth, and marvel at the stained glass windows, which fill the inside with light. Then climb the stairs to the top – if you've got a good head for heights.

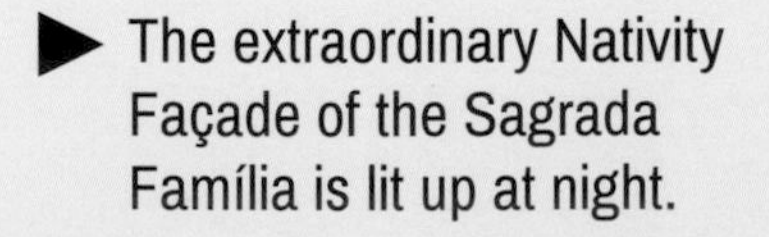

The extraordinary Nativity Façade of the Sagrada Família is lit up at night.

▲ La Boqueria.

Las Ramblas

Las Ramblas is a long, tree-lined avenue that runs through Barcelona, all the way down to the sea. On the way, there are shops, cafés and street performers to keep you entertained. Call in at the bustling La Boqueria – a huge market selling fruit, vegetables, meat and fish. It's where the locals do their shopping. You can stop for a drink and a bite to eat at one of the stalls, or pick up a fruit juice or fruit salad to take away.

▼ The tree-lined street of Las Ramblas.

▲ Barça fans.

Football mad

Football is the most popular sport in Spain, especially in Barcelona. The city is home to one of the world's most famous football clubs – FC Barcelona (known as Barça) – which plays at the Camp Nou Stadium. Barça has won *La Liga* (the Spanish League) 22 times, and the *Copa del Rey* ('King's Cup') 26 times. There are guided tours of the stadium, which can seat around 100,000 fans.

BARCELONA TO PALMA DE MALLORCA

For the last stop on your journey, head for the Balearic Islands – Mallorca, Menorca, Ibiza and Formentera – off the east coast of Spain. Ferries sail from the port in Barcelona to Mallorca, Menorca or Ibiza, or, for a shorter trip, you can catch a plane. Don't forget to pack your swimsuit and suncream – the islands are tourist hotspots, famous for their beautiful beaches and sunny weather.

Mallorca

Mallorca is the largest island with plenty to explore. At the Plaza de España station in Palma, catch the special vintage train to the little town of Sóller on the northwest coast. The train heads into the mountains, through tunnels and across a viaduct. Once you reach Sóller, you can take the tram to the port. The tram used to carry goods from the port, including freshly caught fish packed in ice.

▼ The bustling port of Palma de Mallorca, the capital of Mallorca.

The Caves of Drac are a popular tourist destination.

Caves of Drac

From Sóller, head for the *Cuevas de Drach* (Caves of Drac) on the east coast. These huge caves lie deep underground, together with a vast lake. You can reach the caves down a steep flight of steps, then take a boat ride on the lake. Marvel at the stalactites and stalagmites, and look out for the dragon, once said to live in the caves. *Drach* means 'dragon' in Spanish.

The Sóller tramway has been in use since 1913.

Menorca

Ferries run between the islands and it takes about six hours to reach Menorca. The island is famous for its coastline with around 100 beaches. Almost half of them can only be reached by sea. The best way to explore is by kayak. It takes about ten days to kayak around the whole island, or you can choose a shorter section. The sea around the south coast is less choppy than the north, and you'll find plenty of sandy bays where you can camp overnight.

Tourism

Each year, millions of tourists visit the Balearic Islands, particularly Mallorca. The tourist boom in Mallorca began in the 1950s and is now the island's main source of income. More than half of the islanders work in the tourist business. However, tourism has also brought problems, such as over-use of the island's scarce water supply for hotels and resorts.

GLOSSARY

Antoni Gaudí
Spanish architect who lived from 1852-1926 and specialised in the modernist style. His work often featured nature, including towering tree trunks and animals, such as salamanders. His most famous work, the Sagrada Família in Barcelona, is still unfinished.

aqueduct
A type of bridge built to carry water over a valley or ravine.

Balearics
The islands of Mallorca (Majorca), Menorca, Ibiza and Formentera, which lie off the east coast of mainland Spain.

Basque Country
The name given to the home of the Basque people in the Pyrenees on the border between south-west France and north-east Spain.

Catalan
One of the official languages spoken in parts of north-east Spain, including Barcelona and Girona. It is also the official language of neighbouring Andorra.

choreography
The way in which a dance is designed, planned and set to music, including the movements, steps and patterns of the dancers.

civil war
A war fought between different groups of people living in the same country.

composite volcano
A cone-shaped volcano made from many layers of hardened lava.

crypt
A room or space underneath a church where bodies may be buried.

democracy
A system of government in which people vote for the officials who are going to represent them and in which everyone has a say.

dialects
Forms of language that people speak in different parts of a country, which have different words and grammar to the standard, official language.

dictatorships
Countries ruled by dictators who have absolute power and who often take power by force.

dormant
A volcano that has not erupted for a long time is said to be dormant, or sleeping.

FEVE
Stands for *Ferrocarriles de Vía Estrecha* which is Spanish for 'narrow-gauge railway'. A network of tourist trains that runs along the whole of the north coast.

fiesta
A festival or public celebration in Spain, often held on a religious holiday.

flamenco
A dramatic style of Spanish dance, performed to music.

Galician
A language spoken by more than two million people in Galicia, north-west Spain.

geothermal heat
Heat produced by hot rocks under the ground, in areas of volcanic activity. It can be used to heat water and people's homes.

gorge
A deep, narrow valley with steep sides, usually formed by a river cutting through hard rock.

limestone
A white or grey rock often used as a building material and to make cement.

New World
One of the names used for the Americas (North and South America) by European settlers and explorers when they first discovered them during the 16th century. The 'Old World' was the world they already knew about – Europe, Africa and Asia.

meseta
The high plains, or plateau, in the centre of Spain.

Moors
Muslims who came to Spain from North Africa in the 8th century.

mosques
Places of worship and meeting for Muslims.

Muslims
People who follow the religion of Islam.

pilgrimage
A journey made to a place that is special to a religion, such as a saint's shrine.

sandstone
A type of rock made from tiny fragments of quartz, feldspar and other minerals. It can be pink or yellow in colour and is used in buildings.

stalactites
Columns of rock that hang downwards from the roof of a cave and form over a long period of time.

stalagmites
Columns of rock that grow upwards from the ground in a cave and form over a long period of time.

titanium
A light, strong, white metal.

viaduct
A long, high bridge, held up by many arches, that carries a road or railway over a valley.

BOOKS TO READ

Eyewitness Top 10 Travel Guide: Madrid (Dorling Kindersley, 2015)

The Rough Guide to Spain by Joanna Styles and Simon Willmore (Rough Guides, 2015)

Eyewitness Travel Guide: Spain (Dorling Kindersley, 2014)

Eyewitness Top 10 Travel Guide: Barcelona (Dorling Kindersley, 2014)

Countries Around the World: Spain by Charlotte Guillain (Raintree, 2014)

Lonely Planet: Spain (Travel Guide) by Anthony Ham (Lonely Planet, 2014)

Easy Spanish by Ben Denne and Nicole Irving (Usborne, 2012)

Asterix in Spain by Goscinny and Uderzo (Orion, 2005)

WEBSITES

The Rough Guide to Spain website is packed with interesting and useful information for your visit to Spain. There are tips on where and when to travel, including lots of great itineraries to inspire your own journey around Spain.

http://www.roughguides.com/destinations/europe/spain

Lonely Planet's website is a great introduction to Spain and tells you about the best places to visit, historical and geographical information, food and drink to sample, and offers practical hints and tips about money, health, language and local customs.

http://www.lonelyplanet.com/spain

This website from Michelin provides all the information you'll need for a fascinating and safe journey around Spain. Follow some alternative travel routes, take your pick from loads of travel activities and check out the best places to stay.

http://travel.michelin.com/web/destination/Spain

It's always a good idea to check out the official government advice before you make any journey abroad. You can find out the latest news and information about Spain on this UK government website.

https://www.gov.uk/foreign-travel-advice/spain

Note to parents and teachers:
Every effort has been made by the Publishers to ensure that the websites in this book are suitable for children, that they are of the highest educational value, and that they contain no inappropriate or offensive material. However, because of the nature of the Internet, it is impossible to guarantee that the contents of these sites will not be altered. We strongly advise that Internet access is supervised by a responsible adult.

INDEX